Ancient Egypt and Nubia

Roberta L. Shaw   Krzysztof Grzymski

RŌM

Royal Ontario Museum

First published in 1994 by the Royal Ontario Museum, 100 Queen's Park, Toronto, Ontario M5S 2C6

Editors: Lynn Cunningham, Barbara Ibronyi
Designer: Vickie Vasquez-O'Hara

Canadian Cataloguing in Publication Data
Royal Ontario Museum
    Ancient Egypt and Nubia

(Galleries of the Royal Ontario Museum)
ISBN 0-88854-411-1

1. Egypt - Antiquities - Catalogs. 2. Nubia - Antiquities - Catalogs. 3. Royal Ontario Museum - Catalogs. I. Shaw, Roberta L. (Roberta Lawrie), 1943- . II. Grzymski, Krzysztof A. (Krzysztof Adam), 1951- . III. Title. IV. Series: Royal Ontario Museum. Galleries of the Royal Ontario Museum.

DT59.T67R6 1994   932'.0074'713541   C93-095484-X

Printed and bound in Canada by Friesen Printers

Contents

Predynastic Period
4000–3100 B.C.

← Unification of Egypt

Archaic Period
1st–2nd Dynasty, 3100–2686 B.C.

4th Dynasty, builders of
the three pyramids of →
Giza: 2613–2494 B.C.

Old Kingdom
3rd–6th Dynasty, 2686–2181 B.C.

Fragmentation of →
centralized rule

First Intermediate Period
7th–10th Dynasty, 2181–2040 B.C.

← Reunification under Mentuhotep II

Middle Kingdom
11th–13th Dynasty,* 2040–1674 B.C.

← Hyksos invade Lower Egypt

Second Intermediate Period
14th–17th Dynasty, 1674–1567 B.C.

Hatshepsut's expedition to Punt: about 1500 B.C.
Religious revolution of Akhenaten: about 1375 B.C.
Burial of King Tutankhamun: about 1352 B.C. →
Reign of Ramesses II: 1304–1237 B.C.

New Kingdom
18th–20th Dynasty, 1567–1085 B.C.

Late Period
21st–30th Dynasty and after
1085 B.C.–A.D. 324

Nubian 25th Dynasty: 751–663 B.C.
← Persian conquest: 525 B.C.
Alexander the Great's conquest: 332 B.C.
Roman conquest: 30 B.C.

* 13th Dynasty ends 1633 B.C.

ANCIENT
EGYPT

The name "Egypt" comes from Aigyptos, the ancient Greeks' name for the Nile River from the Mediterranean south to the rapids that formed the natural boundary with Nubia. This name, which dates from the 9th century B.C., may in turn have been a version of Hikuptah, one of the names for Memphis (near modern-day Cairo), the capital of Egypt during the Old Kingdom (2686–2181 B.C.). The civilization that developed along the Nile endured for over 3000 years and accomplished great feats.

The history of the Royal Ontario Museum's Egyptian collection is the story of the creation of the museum itself. In 1902 a keen young Toronto archaeologist, Charles Trick Currelly, was in London conducting research at the British Museum. Through his

Preceding page: **The pyramids at Giza, built during the 4th Dynasty (2613–2494 B.C.).**

work there he met Sir William Matthew Flinders Petrie, considered the father of Egyptian archaeology. Petrie, impressed by Currelly's talents, soon put the young man on the staff of the Egypt Exploration Fund (EEF), which was conducting excavations at Abydos in Upper Egypt.

Just before his departure for Egypt, Currelly was visited by Dr. Nathanael Burwash, chancellor of Toronto's Victoria University. Dr. Burwash urged Currelly to collect artifacts for a privately funded museum to be established at the university—a facility that the prominent Torontonians who were backing the project saw as a resource for the study of Biblical archaeology.

Currelly readily agreed to the plan. The EEF also endorsed the idea, pledging to give some of its finds to the future museum in return for Currelly's work. Among the items donated by the EEF were a number of important artifacts connected with the royal burials of the 1st and 2nd dynasties (3100–2686 B.C.). Today, visitors can view some of these items in the Archaic Period section.

Currelly worked on the Abydos site and others regularly until 1910. In addition to the hundreds of items he secured through his arrangement with the EEF, he was also able to buy many artifacts from local merchants, since at the time these sales were virtually unregulated in Egypt. By 1910 he had amassed more than several thousand artifacts and was back in Toronto devoting his time and energy to creating a home for his collection—the home that was to become the Royal Ontario Museum. Currelly went on to gather many of the Chinese, Greek, Roman, and European items that today can be seen in those respective galleries. In 1914 the museum that began with Currelly's keen interest in Egypt welcomed its first visitors.

HOW THE GALLERY IS ORGANIZED

When the new Egyptian gallery, which opened in January 1992, was being devised, the planners sought the best way to illustrate both the land's long history and daily life in ancient times. The combination of a "history spine" and a "daily-life perimeter wall" enables visitors to enjoy the collection in one walkabout. Like the gallery itself, this guide is designed to give you both a sense of the larger events of history plus an understanding of day-to-day existence in ancient Egypt. Objects in the galleries that are featured in the text are in boldface type, for ease of identification.

THE PREDYNASTIC PERIOD
4000–3100 B.C.

Archaeologists have divided this remote period of Egyptian history into four phases, named after the sites where they were first encountered: Badarian (about 4000 B.C.), Nagada I (4000–3600 B.C.), Nagada II (3600–3200 B.C.), and Nagada III (3200–3100 B.C.).

During the Predynastic phase and even before, Nile Valley inhabitants lived in autonomous villages and sowed crops of barley, flax, and wheat. They kept dogs and raised cattle, sheep, goats, and pigs; the donkey was their beast of burden. Their clothing was of tanned leather and fine linen, and for adornment they strung beads of shell, ivory, carnelian, jasper, and glazed steatite and wore them as bracelets, anklets, and hair ornaments (earrings came much later). They used ground malachite and red ochre to paint their faces and, perhaps, their bodies.

During this time successful irrigation methods resulted in large and prosperous towns, which led to a more complex society. There is evidence that by 3500 B.C. the Nile Valley was organized into a number of centralized chiefdoms. Over the next 300 or 400 years, there continued to be local rulers who controlled the population from a few very large centres. Archaeological excavations at Hieraconpolis (south of modern Luxor), for example, revealed architectural remains of a palace and temple complex.

In the final years of the Predynastic Period, Upper and Lower Egypt represented two distinct cultures. But around 3100 B.C. the cultures were unified under the pharaonic system of government, although Egypt continued to be known as the Two Lands.

Death and Life in the Predynastic Period

No one knows just when ritualistic burial began in Egypt. It was certainly practised throughout the entire Predynastic Period. The **Predynastic burial** at the entrance to the gallery is typical of the simple style common early in this period: the flexed body is wrapped in reed matting and surrounded by simple grave goods, reflecting a belief that possessions and nourishment were needed after death.

Bodies at this time were generally placed in the grave with the face to the west, a direction perhaps associated with ideas about the location of the afterworld. The grave itself would have had a ceiling of branches covered by a low mound of earth. The wooden object lying beside the body may be a weaver's tool; with it the deceased could ply his trade in death as he had in life. The elaborate process of mummification came later; at this time bodies simply dried out in the heat of the desert.

During the following centuries burial practices and funerary religious beliefs became increasingly complex, until they reached the theatrical proportions of the Old Kingdom and later periods. For more on funerary customs and beliefs, see the Religion section, starting on page 36.

Early in the Predynastic Period, most graves, like that of our weaver, contained only a few ordinary items. But as the gap between rich and poor widened, larger and larger tombs containing luxury items became more common. By the end of the Nagada III phase, a feudal class system was firmly established, with peasants, craftsmen, tradesmen, nobles, and, at the pinnacle, the king with his family and close friends.

One striking element of the Predynastic section is the **mourning women,** featured in the case "Early Farmers of the Nile." While some believe they are dancers not mourners, their upraised arms do suggest an attitude of grief, a convention that endured in the depiction of funerals. (The birdlike head of one of the figures is thought to be a simple abstraction rather than symbolism.)

Since far more grave sites than settlements have been discovered, little is known about houses of the Predynastic Period. The **Predynastic house model** was originally suspected of being a forgery because it is unique. Testing proved, however, that it dated from between 4200 and 6400 years ago. It is possible, though, that the red decorative painting was done

Mourning women. Unbaked clay, Predynastic (about 3500 B.C.). Height 36 cm.

early in the 20th century, perhaps to enhance the value of the object.

Food in Ancient Egypt

The source of the River Nile, lifeblood of Egypt, was of little concern to its long-ago inhabitants. But the ancient Egyptians well understood the ways of the river and took advantage of its natural cycle of irrigation and fertilization to produce abundant crops. Each summer, the annual inundation took place, caused by torrential rains far to the south. The Nile would overflow its banks, spreading a thin blanket of rich black soil, washed down from the Ethiopian highlands, onto the fields. Farmers used a series of dykes to keep water from flowing back into the river and so were able to saturate their land enough to produce harvests all through the winter. By June, after the last harvest had been gathered, the river was again at its lowest level, leaving the parched fields—and people—waiting for the flooding once more. (In the south of Egypt, rain was virtually unknown, and in the north it was infrequent and not particularly welcome, since it could literally "melt" the mud-brick homes.)

There were dry years, but an astute system of managing surpluses and shortfalls meant that the population enjoyed a relatively high standard of living. The principal crops sown each fall were wheat and barley, which were used for bread and beer, and flax, which provided linen for clothing. Other

Birth of a calf. Painted wood, early Middle Kingdom (about 2000 B.C.). Height 22 cm.

plants produced oil for cooking, lighting, cosmetics, ointment, and embalming. Kitchen gardens were productive all year, and they yielded onions, garlic, legumes, melons, celery, cucumbers, and lettuce (thought to be an aphrodisiac). Such spices and herbs as cumin, coriander, dill, thyme, and cinnamon were common. Figs, dates, olives, pomegranates, and grapes were also part of the diet, as were fish, fowl, and occasionally meat.

Cattle were raised on the grasslands of the western Delta. The model showing the **birth of a calf**, featured in the "Agriculture" case, is the only three-dimensional treatment of this subject known to have survived from ancient Egypt.

The **Middle Kingdom tomb models** in the "Food and Drink" case illustrate how some food preparation was done. (Wooden models and everyday objects were placed in the tomb to ensure that the dead person would be properly provided with food and services in the afterlife.) The butchering model shows that cattle were trussed before slaughter. In the model, blood is collected from the animal's slit throat and then transferred to a cauldron over burning embers, there to become protein- and iron-rich blood pudding or sausage.

In the kitchen model, a manservant pounds grain with a huge pestle, so that the maidservants behind him can grind the broken grain into fine flour on stone hand mills. Nearby an attendant squats before a container of glowing embers upon which are stacked bread moulds. Many shapes and sizes of bread existed in ancient Egypt; the most common was produced by pouring thin dough into cone-shaped clay moulds that were then stacked and baked. Archaeological sites from this period are positively littered with broken bread moulds. The third man in the scene is forcing partly leavened dough through a sieve into a vat of water, to create a mash that will ferment into nutritious barley beer. Two large sealed beer jars stand at his side, ready for delivery.

THE ARCHAIC PERIOD
3100–2686 B.C., 1st–2nd DYNASTY

Ruling from the first Egyptian capital city of Memphis, the pharaohs of the Archaic Period established a system of government that would last more than 3000 years. Power was centralized in a divine king, whose officials controlled and employed soldiers, craftsmen, and bureaucrats in the service of the state, its gods, and the upper classes.

What would soon become firm traditions of art and learning emerged during this time, the product of the highly specialized craftsmen who served the king and his entourage. Houses (and tombs) were furnished with well-crafted furniture that included beds, chairs, stools, and storage chests, sometimes embellished with **ivory inlay.** Examples of these furnishings are found in the case "Finds from the Early Royal Tombs at Abydos," artifacts that Dr. Currelly was instrumental in acquiring (see pages 6–7). The **gold figurine** in this case, bought by Currelly while in Egypt in the early part of the century, presents an archaeological puzzle. Nothing about the figure looks Egyptian, while certain aspects of it—the facial features, for example—suggest that it may be of early Asiatic origin. Because the clay and cloth core is a modern replacement for the original wood, the figure cannot be tested to determine its age. So while it hints at early contact between Egypt and Asia, there is no way of proving this.

The most distinctive products of the Archaic Period were a vast number of **stone vessels** that set aesthetic standards never to be surpassed by later artisans. Tall concave cylinder jars and squat lug-handled pots exemplify the shapes of this period. Stone sculpture and relief reveal the development of an artistic style that would be firmly entrenched by the 4th Dynasty (2613–2494 B.C.) and would continue until the conquest by Rome in 30 B.C.

THE OLD KINGDOM
2686–2181 B.C., 3rd–6th DYNASTY

Nothing quite so clearly defines Egypt, both ancient and modern, as the three pyramids at Giza, built during the 4th Dynasty. The only surviving example of the ancient Seven Wonders of the World, these overwhelming structures represent the culmination of a rapid expansion of stone-building technology in the service of the royal mortuary cult. This endeavour reached unparalleled grandeur in the Great Pyramid, possibly the most enduring structure that the world has ever known.

Such ambitious undertakings demonstrated a level of stone masonry that was unsurpassed for millennia. The Great Pyramid's four sides are less than a hand's breadth different in length, and the foundation, carved from solid rock, is almost perfectly level. The area covered by its base is slightly over 5 hectares (13 acres), and more than 2 million blocks of stone, each weighing 2.5 tonnes (2.75 tons), were moved to create the largest tomb ever built.

The exact method of construction for this and similar endeavours is still a mystery. The ancient craftsmen and labourers accomplished everything using such basic implements as the **chisels, mauls, and clamps** in the "Building" case. **Plum bobs and boning rods** like those on display were all they used for levelling and sizing, both horizontal and vertical. Simple **architectural sketches** on limestone flakes served as plans for complex monumental buildings.

The building and equipping of the Old Kingdom pyramids represented an enormous state industry, one that channelled much of the country's resources and labour into what was essentially an ancestor cult. These vast complexes also served as large redistribution centres that provided the populace with food and materials as payment for work. Lesser citizens, too, were given elaborate burials, if not on the same scale as those of the pharaohs. Because the ancient Egyptians' idea of eternal life demanded tombs equipped with daily necessities, archaeologists have been able to reconstruct the life of this time. Although the pyramid remained an important symbol in funerary architecture, its size (and exclusivity to royalty) later diminished, until it became merely a "cap" on the tombs of rather ordinary citizens of the New Kingdom (1567–1085 B.C.).

Artistic Achievements

During this period of stability and prosperity there occurred a remarkable flowering of architecture and art. One particularly significant development during the Old Kingdom was what we know today as the canon of proportion. This formula, which was to last almost unchanged throughout the long history of ancient Egypt, was used for both two- and three-dimensional art. It involved a grid system, the basic unit of which was the width of the hand of the human figure being represented. The artist then designed the statue or painting according to the convention that dictated the number of hand-widths necessary to calculate the proportions of other parts of the body. Measuring began at the ground line, and certain points remained constant—the ankle was placed at line 1, for example, while the shoulder fell at line 16. The top of the grid always ended at line 18, which crossed the hairline; this left the artist free to depict hairstyles and headdresses of different heights.

These rules evolved over time, as the notion of the ideal body changed. During the 19th Dynasty (1320–1200 B.C.) in the New Kingdom, line 6 fell at mid-knee rather than at the top of the knee, elongating the leg; by the 20th Dynasty (1200–1085 B.C.) this line was at the lower knee, lengthening the leg even more. During the 25th Dynasty (751–663 B.C.), at the beginning of the Late Period, the grid count changed from 18 to 21 squares, but this made little difference to the overall proportions of the body.

The manner in which the human figure was shown in two-dimensional art was the curious but pleasing combination of front and side views that we think of as typically Egyptian. The **tomb relief of Metjetji** facing the Step Pyramid model provides a good example. The head and face are drawn in profile, except for the eye, which is in front view. The shoulders are full front, while the breast is a combination of front and profile; the body then twists to an almost three-quarter view at the lower abdomen, with the buttocks shown in profile. The arms and legs are in profile, the legs set apart so both can be seen. Hands are presented in front, back, and side views, but feet only in profile, both depicting the inner side with big toe and arch well defined. In the late New Kingdom and occasionally later, the outer side of the foot, showing all five toes, was depicted on the appropriate leg.

Metjetji. Painted limestone relief, 5th Dynasty (about 2400 B.C.). Height 83 cm.

This standardization of art maintained quality in workshop production throughout ancient Egypt. It also led to a high degree of similarity in pieces produced. Diodorus the Sicilian (1st century B.C.) relates a story about two Egyptian sculptors who each made half of a statue, working alone and some distance apart. According to this tale, when the two finished halves were brought together, they fit perfectly.

Unlike Western artists, the Egyptians depicted an object by presenting its most characteristic parts or aspects. Perspective and foreshortening were not part of their style, and they frequently drew groups of animals or people in the overlapping manner of the **relief with donkeys** from Metjetji's tomb. The five donkeys stand in a row along a baseline, one in front of the other, with the nearest figure complete. They are drawn to the same scale and on the same plane. Frequently one figure in a group of otherwise identical figures is given a dramatically different expression, action, or attribute; in the case of this tomb relief, one animal bends its neck to eat from the ground, a position that interrupts the repetition of the grouping and so enhances the balance and interest of the composition. Very often there is an insufficient number of parts for all the figures, as evidenced here—there are only eight front legs for five donkeys. To avoid an unharmonious composition, the artist depicted only the load on the foremost donkey's back, but we are meant to understand that each donkey carries a similar burden. The large sheaf of wheat in front of the donkeys is drawn from above to be at its most recognizable, another common artistic convention.

Most, if not all, sculpture and relief were painted with lively, realistic colours. Paints were derived from such natural pigments as red and yellow ochre, chalk (white), soot (black), or a copper-calcium-silica compound that produced blue and green. The "Artists" case contains examples of **pigments**, some sitting upon **palettes**, on which they were ground to a fine consistency. **Brushes** were made from plant fibres; the ones

Above: Slab with figures. Painted limestone, 18th Dynasty (about 1400 B.C.). Height 39 cm.

Right: Senankh. Painted limestone, 5th Dynasty (about 2400 B.C.). Height 36 cm.

in the case are rather big, suggesting they were used for painting large areas of a single colour.

The **unfinished statuette** in this case represents an early stage in the production of fine stone sculpture. (This particular type, the kneeling figure, was common from the New Kingdom onwards.) Sculptors' training was rigorous and involved the production of many practice pieces, like the elegant **foot** and the **model column.** Because papyrus was much too expensive to be used for drawing practice, limestone chips or pottery sherds, known as ostraca, were employed. Many of these demonstrate great artistic ability, often of a more relaxed nature than the work found in finished tombs and temples. Frequently one or more sketches are superimposed, which suggests that even large flakes were not easily obtained. The teacher's demonstration drawings on the large **slab with figures** at the top of this case includes a partially damaged outline (bottom right) of the earliest known example of a 3-4-5 Pythagorean triangle, produced about 1400 B.C.

THE FIRST INTERMEDIATE PERIOD
2181–2040 B.C., 7th–10th DYNASTY

During the First Intermediate Period the massive pyramid projects came to an end, signalling a decline in the wealth and power of the court at Memphis. The country split into several factions. At the same time there was a climate change, which resulted in many years of inadequate Nile floods, leading to famine and social upheaval. Despite the turmoil, the inhabitants continued to follow their burial traditions, which still reflected a belief in an afterlife. Tombs and their furnishings from this period, however, betray the widespread poverty of the time: not only are there fewer objects, but those that do exist are of markedly lower artistic quality.

In fact, many burials from the First Intermediate Period feature only the quaint **models of houses** that were placed upon the grave in much the same way headstones are used today. These clay models replaced the more elaborate (and expensive) full-sized chapels that were built over graves during the Old Kingdom. Some scholars believe these models represent a type of lower- and middle-class dwelling. The courtyards of the houses contain representations of food offerings for the dead, perhaps as substitutes for the real thing in these hungry years.

THE MIDDLE KINGDOM
2040–1674 B.C., 11th–13th DYNASTY*

A powerful family from the city of Thebes, located on the site of modern Luxor, brought the social chaos and fragmentation of the First Intermediate Period to an end. This family, under Mentuhotep II, triumphed over opposing forces, and so the Two Lands were again united during the 11th Dynasty (about 2040 B.C.). Thebes became the capital of Egypt. The kings of

the 12th Dynasty (1991–1786 B.C.) succeeded in restoring prosperity, in part by taking full advantage of the copper and turquoise mines of Sinai to the west. Egypt extended its control south to Nubia and defended its own borders with massive fortifications, an example of which can be seen in the **Buhen model** in the Nubian Gallery. The rulers of the 12th Dynasty founded a new capital city, Lisht, south of the old capital of Memphis, but continued strong ties with Thebes by supporting the increasingly powerful cult of the god Amun, which was based in Thebes.

As the **model of Mentuhotep II's tomb and mortuary temple** illustrates, this elegant complex departed dramatically from the traditional pyramid style. Located at Deir el-Bahri, across the Nile from Thebes, the temple was a terraced monument of an entirely new kind. Mentuhotep's actual tomb lay deep in the cliff behind the temple and was approached by a long underground tunnel.

* 13th Dynasty ends 1633 B.C.

Although Mentuhotep II was buried about 2010 B.C., his temple remained in use for another 800 years. In the New Kingdom during a short-lived religious revolution under Akhenaten (about 1375 B.C.), many representations of gods were chiselled away (see pages 28–30). Later, kings of the 19th Dynasty sent artists to restore and repaint these images. There is evidence that the **relief of Hathor,** located above the model of Mentuhotep's temple, was among those defaced and later restored. The goddess's facial structure is of a style common in the New Kingdom, and the surrounding stone appears to have been carved away to allow for restoration. Her yellow skin, although a colour often favoured by Egyptian artists for women (red for men), may in this instance portray the gold skin attributed to the gods.

The site of Mentuhotep's temple was excavated by the Egypt Exploration Fund in 1903. Among the party was Dr. Currelly (see pages 6–7). He purchased many artifacts from the temple area, including the fragments of wall reliefs that depict a **procession of court ladies.** Reconstructing this

Tomb figure of Iby-ref. Wood with inlaid eyes, an exquisite example of craftsmanship of the late 12th Dynasty (about 1800 B.C.). Height 46 cm.

Above: Egyptian soldier with axe. Limestone relief, from the temple of Mentuhotep II at Deir el-Bahri, 11th Dynasty (about 2040 B.C.). Height 16 cm.

Left: The goddess Hathor. Painted limestone relief, from the temple of Mentuhotep II at Deir el-Bahri, 11th Dynasty with 19th Dynasty repair (about 2040 and 1300 B.C.). Height 53 cm.

giant jigsaw puzzle was a major challenge for Royal Ontario Museum archaeologists and artists. Bright colours are well preserved on many of the relief fragments in the display. The pigment used for the pastel green of the dresses was probably ground malachite.

The same painstaking effort was required to recreate the **shrine of one of Mentuhotep's wives;** the fragments involved came from one of a series of stone shrines, or tomb chapels, built for six of the king's wives. The aboveground portion of the shrine, shown in the reconstruction, imitated an elaborate wooden cabin with multiple entrances crowned by intricate gratings. The relief decoration commemorated the lady, her royal husband, and her favourite servants.

Today the temple is in ruins. Once the funerary cult of Mentuhotep had lapsed, his temple was gradually dismantled to provide building stone for the projects of subsequent pharaohs, and most of the relief sculptures that once covered the walls from floor to ceiling were destroyed. Sand and fallen rock from the cliff above eventually covered the ruin until the excavation efforts of the Egypt Exploration Fund.

THE SECOND INTERMEDIATE PERIOD
1674–1567 B.C., 14th–17th DYNASTY

The Middle Kingdom came to an end when a rival monarchy of Asiatic settlers established itself in the eastern Delta. These rulers, known as the Hyksos, ultimately controlled all of Lower Egypt. The native kings of the 13th Dynasty (1786–1633 B.C.) were unable to suppress the incursion, and their successors were forced to govern their diminished nation from Thebes. Later Egyptians looked back on this period of foreign domination with shame.

Finally, after years of warfare, the last king of the 17th Dynasty (1650–1567 B.C.), Kamose, and his brother and successor, Ahmose, expelled the Hyksos from the Delta. The **dagger** displayed in the Second

Intermediate Period case bears one of the names of Ahmose, who is regarded as the founder of the 18th Dynasty (1567–1320 B.C.). The weapon closely resembles those found in Hyksos tombs, indicating an Asiatic influence. While the handle and blade are each genuine antiquities, there is some question whether they belong together.

Many innovations were introduced during the years of Hyksos rule. Egyptian soldiers, who had primarily used daggers and war axes, added the **curved Asiatic cutting sword** to their arsenals. The composite bow and the horse and chariot were also adopted by the military. New musical instruments, garden plants, and manufacturing techniques arose, and these soon enhanced the great affluence of the 18th Dynasty.

If you are using this guide in the gallery, you will want to visit the Religion section at this point; see pages 36–43 for related information.

THE NEW KINGDOM
1567–1085 B.C., 18th–20th DYNASTY

The New Kingdom was an exciting period of great military expansion, promoted by a strong central government led by a succession of warrior-kings. The internal prosperity of the country was enriched by tribute from an Egyptian empire that extended into Asia and Africa. Local rulers of Canaan and Syria became vassals, and the Egyptians stationed garrisons in key cities. Nubia was controlled by an Egyptian viceroy called the "Royal Son of Kush," a position second in importance only to the king. Extensive diplomatic and trade contacts were established with these areas, as well as with Aegean and East African cultures, infusing Egyptian life with a new vitality (for a famous royal trading expedition, see "The Punt Wall," pages 33–35).

Artists revived the classic styles of the Old and Middle Kingdoms while adding a grace and delicacy lacking in the earlier art. Egyptian relief and painting reached their highest level in the New Kingdom, with some of the finest work found in the tombs of prominent officials buried at Thebes. Because such tombs were extensively decorated with charming scenes of daily life, so as to ensure its continuation in the afterlife, they have provided us with a wealth of information about the ancient Egyptians.

The case "Early New Kingdom Art" contains an excellent example of this decorative art in the fragment that depicts **men bringing offerings to a funeral** from the tomb of Nebamun and Ipuky. The offerings consist of lotus flowers and ointment carried by the son and father-in-law of Ipuky. Nebamun and Ipuky were both married to the same woman, but it is uncertain which man died first. Both men were super-

Men bringing offerings. Painted plaster, from the tomb of Nebamun and Ipuky, 18th Dynasty (about 1400 B.C.). Height 28 cm.

visors in the royal workshops, scenes of which were painted on the tomb walls at Thebes. That this women was able to dedicate such a tomb suggests she was a person of independent wealth.

There are two types of ancient Egyptian murals. The first, like that of the offering bearers, was sketched and then painted on a flat surface. The second type was carved in low relief before being painted: an example is the **hunting scene,** at the top of the case. The complete scene would have shown the owner of the tomb engaged in the popular sport of hunting with bow and arrow. The arrow visible through the flesh of the neck of the fox (lower right) is an example of "false transparency," an artistic convention in which an object is seen in its entirety, even though in reality this would be impossible. Scattered compositions like those in this relief were used only in hunting or battle scenes, to represent the chaos and action of those pursuits; in more ordered scenes, the subjects are placed firmly on a baseline, often neatly arranged in balanced registers. Traces of the original paint remain on this piece, and dots on the background indicate a desert terrain, which the Egyptians associated with ideas of chaos and hostility.

The opulence associated with ancient Egypt reached its peak during the 18th Dynasty. This was the era of the famous King Tutankhamun, whose tomb furnishings characterize that affluence. Personal adornment was sumptuous: elaborate wigs and hairstyles, colourful jewellery, perfumed cosmetics, and elegant clothing were common. Jewellery was worn by everyone, even pets: the "Jewellery" case contains a **child's necklace, anklets, amulet, and earring** as well as a **cat's necklace.** A fine example of a typical ornament worn for special occasions is the **broad collar** mounted on the wall. The offering bearers who appear on the fragment in the case "Early New Kingdom Art" also wear these necklaces.

Earrings did not come into vogue until the 18th Dynasty, and although men certainly wore them—

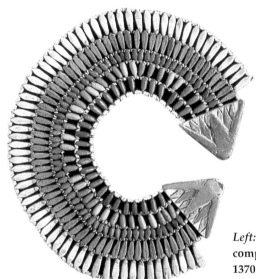

Left: Broad collar. Faience (glazed composition), 18th Dynasty (about 1370 B.C.). Diameter 19 cm.

Far left: Mirror with girl holding kitten. Bronze, New Kingdom (1567–1085 B.C.). Height 24 cm.

King Tutankhamun had many pairs—men are seldom depicted wearing them in paintings and sculpture. The size of earrings varied a great deal; the pair of **ivory studs** that are part of the display would have demanded a very large hole in the earlobe. An item exclusively for women was the **girdle,** which was placed low on the hips and generally adorned the naked body, although occasionally it might be worn under sheer robes.

True gemstones—diamonds, rubies, sapphires—were unknown to the Egyptians. They valued such semiprecious stones as turquoise, carnelian, feldspar, red jasper, and, above all, lapis lazuli, which was imported from what is today Afghanistan. During the Predynastic Period they developed a substance of powdered quartz that was glazed, which today is known as faience. Using this paste they imitated the colours of the more expensive stones and often mixed the two in a piece of jewellery. Even Tutankhamun's jewels are a mixture of "fake" and "real."

The Amarna Style

The pharaoh Akhenaten, who ruled from 1379 to 1362 B.C., instituted a religious revolution, substituting a single sun god, the Aten, for the many gods of former times (see pages 36–38). This "heretic king" moved the capital north from Thebes to Amarna, and here he inspired a change in art that broke with many of the old conventions. The new approach, known today as the Amarna style, emphasized free curving lines, expressive poses, and naturalistic forms and tended toward an exaggerated realism that often came close to caricature. The free use of curved lines enabled the artist to depict the **boy bringing provisions** in the case "Art of the Amarna Period" in an almost sketchlike fashion, successfully reflecting the awkwardness of his heavy load and the haste with which he hurries to complete his delivery. The shape of the head, the treatment of the face, and the rounded belly are typical of the Amarna style. The sunk relief, also typical of this period, was faster to work up than the more laborious raised relief of earlier times and suggests a flurry of building activity in the new city of Amarna.

Artists did retain a certain elegance in the portrayal of the royal family, as seen in the **relief of King Akhenaten and Queen Nefertity** worshipping the Aten. The fragments in this case come from temples that were dismantled at Akhenaten's death, when the monotheism he imposed was outlawed, and the old religion reinstated. For a time, some of the Amarna traits lingered, but eventually artists returned to the older, more restrained and conventional style, as

King Akhenaten and Queen Nefertity. Limestone and plaster, 18th Dynasty (about 1375 B.C.). Height 38 cm.

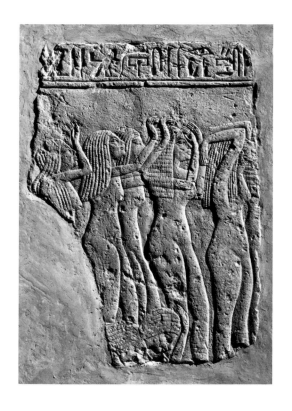

reflected in the objects of the case "Late New Kingdom Art." Note **the mourning women relief fragment** from the **tomb of Maya,** an official whose tenure spanned both the Amarna and the post-Amarna eras. The grouping of the figures, the roundness of the forms, and the freedom of the gestures retain some of the naturalistic Amarna spirit. The **fragment** from the **tomb of Tjia** represents the mother, sister, and brother-in-law of Ramesses II of the 19th Dynasty, often referred to as Ramesses the Great.

Mourning women. Limestone relief, from the tomb of Maya, 18th Dynasty (about 1360 B.C.). Height 46 cm.

THE LATE PERIOD
1085 B.C.–A.D. 324, 21st–30th DYNASTY

The latter years of the New Kingdom were marked by a disintegration of traditional government that once again resulted in a breakdown of power and the loss of the empire. The time of the 21st to the 24th Dynasty is often referred to as the Third Intermediate Period (1085–715 B.C.), because it was characterized by political fragmentation. While open conflict rarely occurred, there were strong independent factions in Lower and Upper Egypt; high officials were effective only within their regional territories. When kings tried to maintain power by establishing members of their families in these provincial centres, the result was often the creation of semi-independent royal houses.

By 715 B.C. the Kushites, or Nubians, who had established themselves as the 25th Dynasty, completed their conquest of Egypt. The finely carved **scarab commemorating the Kushite victory** proclaims

Scarab of King Shabako. Glazed steatite, 25th Dynasty (about 710 B.C.). Height 9 cm.

the victory of the Kushite king Shabako over Egyptian rebels, foreign peoples, and "sand dwellers" (of the Levant), who, fighting among themselves, delivered each other up as prisoners. Dr. Currelly purchased this piece in 1910 in Jerusalem, and for many years scholars (none of whom had ever seen it) considered it

31

to be a forgery. In 1956, however, after intensive study by a distinguished French Egyptologist, the scarab was declared genuine and now ranks as one of the museum's most interesting artifacts, because of the rarity of such royal items.

The Kushites were not able to overcome the fragmented political structure of Egypt or to resist increasing Assyrian pressure from the east. The 26th Dynasty (663–525 B.C.), the last great era of pharaonic history, reunified the country and again centralized the government at Memphis. At the end of the 26th Dynasty, Egypt succumbed to Persian domination.

Artists, nostalgic for the glorious past, tried to imitate the art of earlier ages and in many instances made direct copies of existing material. For example, many of the charming mural scenes in the 18th Dynasty tombs at Thebes were duplicated in tombs of the 26th

Bokennenife. Greywacke, 27th Dynasty (about 500 B.C.). Height 49 cm.

Dynasty. A good example of this revival of the old style is the well-executed kneeling figure of the **royal scribe Bokennenife** in the case "Art of the Late Period." It represents an elderly man presenting an image of the god Ptah to the temple as an act of piety and reverence. The hieroglyphic dedication asks Ptah to grant the man prosperity, continued piety, and long life.

After a final brief period of independence, the country fell to Alexander the Great in 332 B.C. His general Ptolemy assumed power in Egypt in 323 B.C., establishing a Macedonian dynasty that ably ruled until the famous and brilliant Cleopatra VII was overcome by the Roman general Octavius (later Augustus Caesar) in 30 B.C. During the Ptolemaic Period, artists maintained Egyptian traditions for sculpture in the round; the life-size bust of a **Ptolemaic queen or goddess** shows no trace of classical Greek influence. The unfinished **triad stela,** also dating to this period, honours the Theban gods Amun, Mut, and Khonsu, as well as Re, Shu, and Tefnut, gods connected with the city of Heliopolis, one of Egypt's very early cult centres. The stela reflects a serious attempt on the part of the Ptolemaic pharaohs to embrace attributes of Egyptian kingship out of respect for the long traditions of their adopted country.

THE PUNT WALL

The great Queen Hatshepsut of the 18th Dynasty was a powerful woman who reigned alone as pharaoh of Upper and Lower Egypt from 1503 to 1482 B.C. In the ninth year of her reign, she mounted a large trading expedition to the fabled country of Punt, a region famous for its incense that is thought to have been situated along the coastline of present-day Somalia. Egyptians of the time also called Punt "the Land of God," which they imagined as a distant and enchanted place with precious incense trees, fabulous beasts, and wonderful riches.

The Punt wall commemorates this historic journey; the museum's version was cast from the original relief murals of the mortuary temple of Hatshepsut, located at Deir el-Bahri on the west bank of the Nile at Thebes. The architecture of her temple reflects a heavy influence from that of the temple of Mentuhotep II, built 500 years earlier, just to the south. The casting was done in 1906 and 1907 by Dr. Currelly, who was able to persuade a group of prominent Torontonians who visited him in Egypt to finance the colouring by a professional artist.

Hatshepsut was succeeded by her hostile nephew Thutmose III, who defaced her images after her death. Such destruction can be seen in the large erased figure, which showed the queen celebrating the triumphant return of her ships. She and her smaller spirit-double are depicted as men, because Hatshepsut was officially a king like other kings.

Left: **Unidentified queen or goddess. Granite, early Ptolemaic (323–200 B.C.). Height 63 cm. In the background is the Punt wall.**

RELIGION OF ANCIENT EGYPT

THE GODS

The Egyptians had no single view of the meaning of life or of the divine. Their religion involved the worship of several hundred gods, each having a local cult centre, many of which had existed since Predynastic times. The ancient towns incorporated, rather than eliminated, each other's gods as the country moved toward unification, leaving the people with a hodge-podge of deities and no required set of beliefs.

In time, many cult centres adopted some practices of other cults. Sometimes two gods became one or were thought to have married one another; these blendings or alliances created links among many centres. As power shifted in the course of Egyptian history, the deities of the dominating city assumed the leading role. Some of these images are included in the case "Gods and Goddesses." One of the oldest local groups was the **gods of Memphis,** where the creator god **Ptah** was worshipped along with his consort, **Sakhmet,** and their son, **Nefertem,** and where the **Apis bull** was honoured.

Amun, originally a local god worshipped at Thebes, first gained prominence during the 11th Dynasty. By about 1500 B.C. he and the sun-god, Re, had become one and headed the Egyptian pantheon as Amun-re, king of the gods. During the New Kingdom, temples were built to him throughout the empire.

Many of the gods were represented as animals or even as human forms with animal heads. This does not mean that the Egyptians thought of such gods as being animals, or even that they worshipped animals. Rather, they seemed to see a sense of the divine in life itself, as well as the sources of life—the sun, the Nile—and so all such forms were somehow worked into their spiritual scheme.

Although Egyptian religion was without real dogma, the many gods provided a means to express the mystery and sanctity of life and death and a faith

The goddess Neith. Bronze, 26th Dynasty (about 600 B.C.). Height 36 cm.

in an ideal universal order that embodied truth, harmony, and justice. This order or stability was a recurring theme in the religious literature, and the concept itself was personified in the goddess Maat. The gods themselves were involved in a constant effort to maintain this order or, frequently, to restore it after some chaotic event.

THE KING

Interposed between the gods and humans was the king, also regarded as a god, yet subordinate to the other divinities, to whom he was responsible for maintaining Maat on earth. This notion was reinforced in a ritual in which the **pharaoh offered a symbol or figure of Maat** to the gods. In return, they ensured ultimate victory over foreign enemies, whose aggression signified the dissolution of Maat, resulting in chaos. Often upon his succession to the throne, a pharaoh would proudly proclaim that he had restored Maat, implying, of course, that his predecessor had let it slip.

For one brief period about 1375 B.C., the long-held system of beliefs was abruptly and drastically altered by a religious revolution instigated by the pharaoh Akhenaten. He declared the sun itself, which he called the Aten, to be the supreme and sole god of Egypt and closed the shrines of the traditional gods. The royal family worshipped the Aten directly, while the people worshipped the god through their king. After Akhenaten's death, the old gods were reinstated and their temples refurbished. The Aten's temples were demolished and used for building purposes, and Akhenaten's name was deleted from the records.

THE TEMPLE

An Egyptian temple was the focus of ritual, the "god's house" where the deity lived in the form of a cult image.

In the huge national shrines, professional and lay priests anointed and dressed the image daily, made offerings of food, and burned sweet-smelling incense. On festival occasions, the cult image was carried out of the temple in public procession. Because music was thought to please the gods and banish evil, priestess-musicians chanted, shook their metal rattles (known as **sistra**), and clapped their **castanets** in lively fashion (these objects can be seen in the "Temples" case). These processions allowed the common people a sense of closeness to their god, for only the king and the high priests were allowed to enter the inner sanctum of the temple, where a mystic union between the king and the god was believed to take place.

THE AFTERLIFE

People whose lives had been spent in accordance with Maat could expect that after death they would go on living in a new eternal life. Although mummification was not a strict requirement for resurrection in the next world, it was certainly seen as a highly desirable method of attaining that status.

The Egyptian belief system viewed a human being as having three components: the physical "mechanical" body and two non-physical, or spiritual, aspects that remain rather obscure to us today (and probably were to the ancient Egyptians as well). One they called the *ka*, which represented the life force within the shell of the body. Although it was released and separated at death, it was somehow anchored to the remaining (mummified) body, dependent upon it for its continuing existence, which is why food offerings were placed in tombs. A popular toast at social gatherings was "To your *ka*." The second spiritual element was the *ba*, which represented an individual's character and personality. This, too, was separated at death and strove to reunite with the *ka*, to make a successful transition to everlasting life.

In order to attain the desired afterlife, it was important to follow traditions that included mummification, protection of and sustenance for the body through an appropriately equipped and maintained tomb, and support for the spiritual aspects through formal funerary liturgy.

Mummies remain a fascinating signature of the culture of ancient Egypt. In its fully developed state in the New Kingdom, mummification involved an expensive method of embalming the body using soda (natron), spices, and resins in a procedure that could take up to 70 days. The internal organs were removed, the body desiccated in natron, the cavities (and sometimes the face and limbs) packed, and the body posed. The removed organs—the liver, lungs, stomach, and intestines—were generally separately preserved and stored in a set of four **canopic jars** that were placed next to the coffin in the tomb; an example is included in the display containing the **mummy-case of Djed-maatesankh.** Linen bandages were wrapped around the extremities and then around the entire body. Ritual prayers accompanied each stage of the process, during which **amulets** and a **heart scarab** might be inserted into the bandaging; the scarab was a very important funerary accessory that was inscribed with a spell from the "Book of the Dead" that essentially prevented the heart (which was left in the body) from testifying against itself during the final judgement in the next world.

The New Kingdom "Book of the Dead" consisted of some 200 spells, usually written and illustrated on papyrus. These were designed to aid the deceased in making a successful transition to the next life, and the Egyptians knew them collectively as "The Book of Coming Forth in the Daytime." The most important spell was that on the heart scarab. A person (or the family) would choose a number of spells that most appealed to the individual to accompany him to the tomb, in the form of a rolled-up papyrus.

After the body was appropriately wrapped, a

mummy mask was sometimes placed on the body before it was put into a decorated coffin like the **mummy-case with the mummy of Antjau.** This mummy was brought to Toronto late in the 19th century and, in keeping with late Victorian romanticism, was for years known as the Lady Hatasis. In 1952, however, Winifred Needler, then the Egyptian curator of the Royal Ontario Museum, discovered that the coffin was that of a man named Antjau. The label was quietly changed, but a newspaper reporter noticed the switch. The resulting story—"Princess of the Nile Now a Man!"—caught the attention of several North American newspapers, which at the time were full of news about a sensational sex-change operation.

The **mummy-case of Djedmaatesankh** is a beautiful example of a casing made of glue-soaked linen.

Mummy-case of Djedmaatesankh with canopic jars. Moulded and plastered cloth, 22nd Dynasty (about 850 B.C.); limestone, Late Period (about 850 B.C.). Height of mummy-case 165 cm.

The wrapped and mummified body was inserted through the slit in the back. A thin layer of gesso-plaster was applied and then painted when dry with the appropriate funerary iconography for the protection and sustenance of the body. The face has been covered with gold leaf to symbolize the godly state the person has attained. This kind of case would be put into one or more decorated coffins.

Just below the outstretched wings on her chest is a depiction of the deceased, dressed in her fine linen dress, being led into the presence of Osiris, supreme god of the afterlife, who is seated on a throne. The scales behind her signify that she has passed the final judgement, wherein her heart is weighed against a feather, the symbol of Maat, and she will therefore gain entry into the afterlife. X-rays show that the body's bandages contain at least two of the amulets that custom prescribed: a vulture with protective outstretched wings resting upon the upper chest (probably made of sheet gold), and a large heart scarab, no doubt inscribed with the requisite spell from a "Book of the Dead."

In late Egyptian times, and to a lesser extent in the New Kingdom, animals were raised in the temple precincts and, when they died, mummified and buried in subterranean chambers of the temple. Thousands of ibis mummies were found in such chambers at Saqqara (south of Giza) and Hermopolis (north of Amarna). The birds and other animals (including some insects) were considered sacred to the god they represented, and some, such as the hawk and the cat, became protected species throughout Egypt. It was considered a pious act to pay for the burial of a sacred animal. The intricate wrappings of the **animal mummies** are deceptive—often inside such a splendid specimen lies only a jumble of bones that may not even make up a complete skeleton of the creature or may contain several extra bones.

An imposing and extremely rare artifact, the **funerary bed of Herty** represents a very late survival (perhaps as late as the 3rd century A.D.) of private funerary painting and hieroglyphic script. While the gods are shown in profile—the traditional Egyptian style—Herty and his wife face forward in the Roman fashion and wear Roman clothes. This kind of bed frequently appears in paintings of funeral processions, where it supports the coffin or sarcophagus during transport to the tomb. Because so few actual examples have survived, it is supposed that they were not left in tombs; however, three examples were found in the tomb of King Tutankhamun—perhaps a royal prerogative.

The cast of the **tomb chapel of Kitines,** which dates from the same period as the bed, also represents the last vestiges of the traditional funerary religion. The casting, made possible by the Egyptian government, was painted to represent the present-day colour. In antiquity, these reliefs would have been painted in the customary colourful manner.

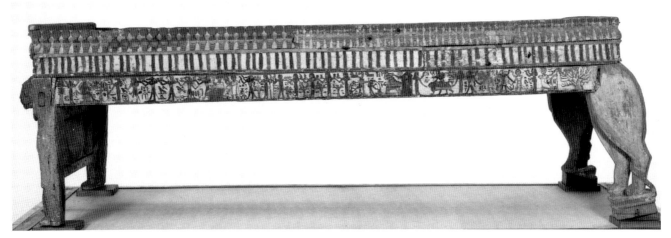

Funerary bed of Herty. Plastered and painted wood, Roman Period (A.D. 100–300). Height 67 cm.

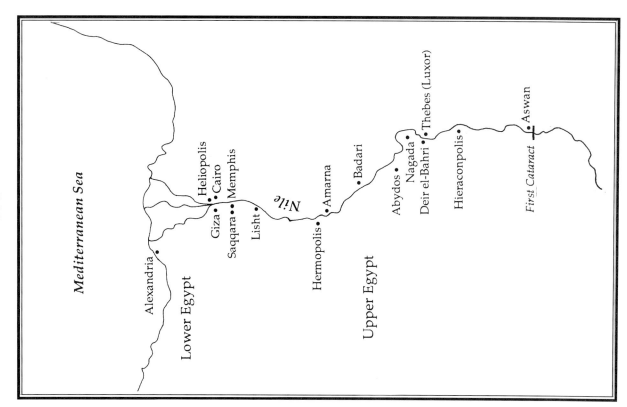

Egypt

Mediterranean Sea

Lower Egypt

Upper Egypt

Alexandria

Heliopolis
Giza • Cairo
Saqqara • • Memphis
Lisht

Nile

Hermopolis • Amarna

• Badari

Abydos
Nagada •
Deir el-Bahri • • Thebes (Luxor)

Hieraconpolis

First Cataract + • Aswan

Nubia and Central Sudan

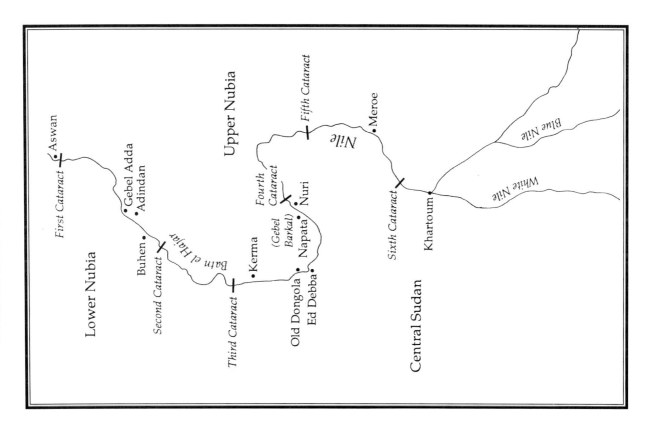

Lower Nubia

Upper Nubia

Central Sudan

First Cataract
• Aswan

Gebel Adda
• Adindan

Buhen •

Second Cataract

Batn el Hajar

Third Cataract

• Kerma

(Gebel Barkal)
Napata
• Nuri

Fourth Cataract

Old Dongola •
Ed Debba •

Fifth Cataract

Nile

• Meroe

Sixth Cataract

• Khartoum

Blue Nile

White Nile

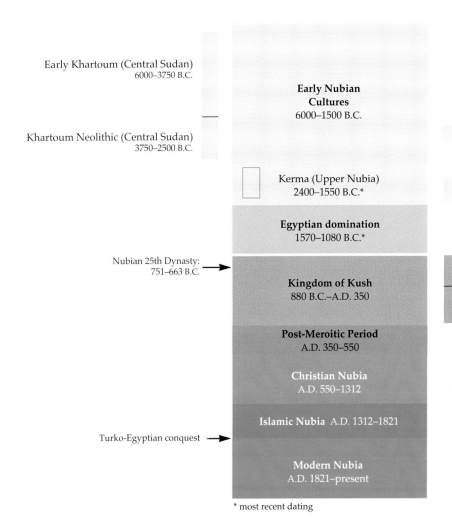

Early Khartoum (Central Sudan)
6000–3750 B.C.

Khartoum Neolithic (Central Sudan)
3750–2500 B.C.

**Early Nubian
Cultures**
6000–1500 B.C.

A-Group (Lower Nubia)
3400–2900 B.C.

Kerma (Upper Nubia)
2400–1550 B.C.*

C-Group (Lower Nubia)
2250–1500 B.C.

12th Dynasty occupation of
Lower Nubia: 1991–1786 B.C.

Kerma culture occupation of
Lower Nubia: 1786–1550 B.C.

Egyptian domination
1570–1080 B.C.*

Nubian 25th Dynasty:
751–663 B.C.

Kingdom of Kush
880 B.C.–A.D. 350

Napatan Period, 880–300 B.C.

Meroitic Period, 300 B.C.–A.D. 350

Post-Meroitic Period
A.D. 350–550

Christian Nubia
A.D. 550–1312

Islamic Nubia A.D. 1312–1821

Turko-Egyptian conquest

Modern Nubia
A.D. 1821–present

* most recent dating

NUBIA AND THE NUBIANS

B etween Khartoum in Sudan and Aswan in Egypt, the Nile weaves and winds through the land known as Nubia. Every now and then the smooth flow of the river is interrupted by a series of granite rock outcrops called cataracts. The First Cataract, near Aswan, forms a natural as well as a cultural boundary between Egypt and Nubia. The area between the First Cataract and the inhospitable Batn el Hajar (Arabic for "Belly of Rocks"), just south of the Second Cataract, is called Lower Nubia. Here the Nile forms a narrow valley between the hills and cliffs of red sandstone, with small patches of cultivable land. Further south, in Upper Nubia, the landscape changes dramatically to wide open spaces, with the arable land bordered by the desert. Only in the areas of the Third, Fourth,

Preceding page: **The pyramid field at Nuri, where the Napatan kings were buried between 664 and 300 B.C.**

Fifth, and Sixth cataracts does the Nile Valley narrow once more, creating a landscape somewhat like parts of Lower Nubia. The most southerly parts of Nubia, now Central Sudan, lie within the rain belt, which meant that inhabitants were less dependent on the river and its annual flood. Savannah-like grass predominates here, and acacia trees are abundant. Because of these geographical and climatic differences, Nubia and Central Sudan's history is quite unlike Egypt's. While that country remained culturally and ethnically homogeneous for 3000 years, various parts of Nubia were inhabited by different peoples at different times.

Today the southern limit of the Nubian-speaking population is near Ed Debba, halfway between the Third and the Fourth cataracts, but in medieval times the Nubians occupied the whole length of the Nile Valley between Aswan and the northern reaches of

Rocky, desolate landscape of Lower Nubia near the Second Cataract.

Acacia trees growing densely in Central Sudan at Meroe.

the Blue and the White Niles. Greek and Roman writers mentioned tribes such as the Noba and Nobatae (or Nobadae), from whom the modern name of the country is probably derived, although some scholars believe it comes from an ancient Egyptian word for gold: *nub*. The Greeks and Romans used the name Ethiopia, rather than Nubia, to describe lands south of Egypt, and to the ancient Egyptians Nubia was Ta-Seti ("Land of the Bow").

Another popular Egyptian term was Kush, which was probably first applied to the Kerma Kingdom that flourished in Upper Nubia during the Middle Kingdom (2040–1674 B.C.). Later, the name became synonymous with all of Nubia and was used even by its own rulers between 880 B.C. and A.D. 350.

THE REDISCOVERY OF NUBIA

The erection of the High Dam at Aswan in the early 1960s meant the flooding of all of Lower Nubia. But before that happened, a period of intense archaeological activity made Lower Nubia one of the best-explored regions in the world.

The story of Upper Nubia and Central Sudan is entirely different: because only a handful of sites have ever been excavated there, our knowledge remains limited. New sites and whole new cultures are still being discovered by archaeologists, including researchers from the Royal Ontario Museum.

EARLY CULTURES
6000–1500 B.C.

In 1944 excavations at the site of the Khartoum Hospital revealed the remains of a culture known as Early

Khartoum, or Khartoum Mesolithic (6000–3750 B.C.). The items discovered included **pottery decorated with wavy lines,** tiny stone tools that archaeologists call **microliths, bone harpoons,** and grinding **stones.** Although seemingly unimpressive, these modest objects indicate their owners' successful adaptation to the local environment.

The Early Khartoum site offered evidence that not all early societies that used pottery and grinding stones lived in villages and engaged in farming. Here the people were hunter-gatherers who lived in semi-permanent settlements and collected wild grains and vegetables, gathered molluscs, fished, and hunted wild animals. They only began to breed such animals as sheep, goats, and cattle during the Khartoum Neolithic Period (3750–2500 B.C.).

In Central Sudan, the 2000 years following the Neolithic era represent a puzzle, for archaeologists have so far failed to discover any evidence of human occupation there. The same is not true of the northern regions, where George A. Reisner, an early 20th-century archaeologist, identified a series of cultures. The earliest one, which he called the A-Group, flourished between 3400 and 2900 B.C. The A-Group people lived in small camps, grew some grains, kept domesticated animals, and traded extensively with Egypt. Among the many types of clay vessels produced by the A-Group people, the beautifully decorated, thin-walled eggshell wares, like the **painted conical bowl,** are most striking.

The C-Group culture (2250–1500 B.C.), which succeeded the A-Group in Lower Nubia after a gap of several hundred years, produced distinctive **black bowls and cups** with incised decoration filled with white paste. The contemporary Kerma culture, so-named for an archaeological site near the Third Cataract, produced handmade vessels so thin that early archaeologists believed that they were made on a potter's wheel. The case "Kingdom of Kerma" contains **tulip-shaped red beakers** with a wide black

Nubian pottery through the ages. *Left to right:* Eggshell bowl, A-Group (about 3000 B.C.). Tulip-shaped beaker, Kerma (1600 B.C.), on loan from the Museum of Fine Arts, Boston. Amphora, Meroitic (about A.D. 100). Footed goblet, post-Meroitic (about A.D. 350). Vase, Late Christian (about A.D. 1150). Sgraffito bowl, Mameluke (about A.D. 1400). Height of bowl on far left 18.5 cm.

band around the rim that are perhaps the most typical example of Kerma ceramics.

The differences between the C-Group and Kerma cultures go beyond the types of pottery they produced. C-Group people seem to have been partly herders and partly farmers living in camps and villages, where they sometimes used stone slabs for wall and house construction. Kerma, however, was an urbanized, multiclass society whose rulers were buried in monumental tombs. The remains of the walled city of Kerma are still impressive today, especially the structure now known as the Deffufa, which probably served as the main temple.

EGYPT AND NUBIA
2400–1080 B.C.*

Despite its harsh climate and often inhospitable landscape, Nubia was always of great interest to the Egyptians, primarily because of its natural resources. From Old Kingdom times (and perhaps earlier) Egyptians were quarrying Nubian granite, basalt, diorite, and other hard stones and mining copper ore. They were also importing the skins of African animals, ostrich feathers, ivory, and ebony, and some of these goods were clearly brought from the lands beyond Nubia. The ultimate treasure, however, was the gold found in the Nubian desert and the Red Sea hills.

Occasional trade and military expeditions to Nubia eventually led to the complete occupation of Lower Nubia at the time of the 12th Dynasty (1991–1786 B.C.). Control of Lower Nubia was regained by the Kerma rulers during the Second Intermediate Period (1674–1567 B.C.). The New Kingdom pharaohs (1567–1085 B.C.) successfully fought the Kushites of Kerma and eventually extended their empire all the way up the Nile to the Fourth Cataract. There, a magnificent temple for the god Amun was built at the foot of Gebel Barkal (or Napata), consid-

* most recent dating

54

ered by the Egyptians to be sacred and known as "Pure Mountain." For five centuries Nubia remained under Egyptian control, ruled by a viceroy whose title was the "Royal Son of Kush" and whose rank was among the highest in the court.

KINGDOM OF KUSH:
NAPATA AND MEROE
880 B.C.–A.D. 350

The collapse of the Egyptian Empire after 1085 B.C. gave Nubia independence, but because archaeological and historical information does not exist for the next two centuries, we are not sure what was going on. There is also no way of knowing whether the native Kushite people and their rulers who occupied the city of Napata following these dark ages were in any way related to the Kerma people. We do know that within a short period of time the Napatan kings extended their power from Nubia to the Mediterranean coast, ruling Egypt as the 25th Dynasty (751–663 B.C.). Even though clearly influenced by Egyptian culture and customs, they preferred to be buried near Napata. There, at the burial grounds Kurru and Nuri, the kings and pharaohs were interred under small pyramids built of sandstone blocks. Their tombs included large numbers of objects, such as Egyptian-style **shawabti figurines.** The case "Rise of the Kushite Empire" contains nine examples of these figures, which were generally equipped with hoes and a basket for moving dirt, so as to enable the shawabti to do field work in place of the deceased in the afterlife.

We do not know why the royal burial grounds were transferred south to Meroe after 300 B.C. At the same time the use of Egyptian motifs in art and architecture declined, and Meroitic replaced Egyptian as the language of inscriptions. The mystery of Meroitic writing is one of the most intriguing problems in Nubian history and archaeology. The Meroites

adapted 23 Egyptian signs to write their own language, and in the early 20th century the Welsh scholar Francis Llewellyn Griffith identified phonetic values of individual characters. But while we can now read the texts, the meaning of the words still eludes us.

The Meroites continued to worship such Egyptian gods as Isis (known as Wosa), Osiris (known as Asore), and Amun (known as Amani), but the cult of a local lion-headed warrior-god, Apedemak, gained importance. While the Kushites shared some of the funerary customs of the Egyptians, they had others that were uniquely Nubian. For example, they did not mummify their dead, except perhaps for the members of the royal family. Instead, the bodies were wrapped in shrouds and placed on beds—a tradition going back to Kerma times—and funerary stelae and offer-

Left to right: **Shawabti figurines of King Anlamani, Queen Madiqen, and King Aspalta. Faience, Napatan (620–560 B.C.). Height of shawabti on left 26 cm.**

ing tables were often placed in front of the grave. In Lower Nubia there was also a custom of including a statue representing the soul of the deceased, known as the *ba*. The **ba-statue** in the first "Kushite Empire" case has the typical human body with bird's wings. Sometimes these statues depict a bird with a human head.

Dozens of Meroitic cemeteries were discovered and explored during the Nubian salvage campaign, but very few town sites have been studied. The two capital cities of Napata and Meroe are still only partially excavated. The ruins of Meroe cover hundreds of hectares, making the site one of the largest in Africa. Parts of the royal compound at Meroe were unearthed by British archaeologists between 1909 and 1914; palaces and a pool surrounded by **statuary** were found—possibly a royal bath. A 1972–1984 joint expe-

Column base with reliefs of lions and rams. Faience, from Meroe (about A.D. 100). Height 37 cm. A rare example of a faience object of this size.

dition sponsored by the universities of Calgary and Khartoum made a most important discovery: iron-smelting furnaces. Their existence confirmed Meroe's role as a major industrial centre of the ancient world. Among the items displayed are **iron nails, hooks, and arrowheads** as well as **clay bellows nozzles.**

The Meroitic potters continued the traditions of their predecessors, producing attractively decorated vessels of outstanding quality. In addition to traditional geometric and floral motifs, animals and humans were often depicted on **amphorae** and **vases.** The large vessels the potters produced were used for such liquids as wine, beer, and oils as well as for dry goods. Amphorae from western North Africa, southern France, and Anatolia have been found in the royal tombs at Meroe, an indication that the Meroites actively participated in the international trade network that flourished in the early centuries A.D.

DIVIDED KINGDOMS: THE POST-MEROITIC PERIOD
A.D. 350–550

After the centuries of unified rule by the kings of Kush, Nubia became divided into several small kingdoms. This end of the Napatan-Meroitic civilization coincided with the fall of the Roman Empire. The Byzantine successors of Rome had dealings with the new political and ethnic groups in Nubia, as is clear from the accounts of Byzantine writers and from a new pottery style that emerged at this time. During this period, Lower Nubia was settled by the Blemmye and the Nobatae tribes, while in the south the Noba people played the main role.

These post-Meroitic warrior-kings continued trading, and fighting, with the north and the south, as is clear from the grave finds. The **footed goblets** from Lower Nubia and **large bulbous jars** from Upper Nubia and Central Sudan are the most characteristic examples of the pottery of the period. Those in the "Divided Kingdoms" cases are thought to be connected with the Bacchic cults that were common at the time.

The 1962–1966 excavations at Gebel Adda, conducted by N. B. Millet, now a Royal Ontario Museum curator, uncovered thousands of clay vessels as well as excellently preserved leather goods such as **quivers and sandals, glass bottles, bronze bowls, iron swords and knives,** and many other artifacts. The cases "Economy," "Household," and "Arts, Crafts, Adornments" contain examples. The National Geographic Society, which financed the project, generously donated its share of finds to the museum. The site of Gebel Adda was continuously occupied from the Late Meroitic Period until the 16th century, and apart from the post-Meroitic material, many artifacts of the Meroitic, Christian, and Islamic periods were also found and are displayed in these three cases.

Imported and local glassware. From Gebel Adda (A.D. 200–550). Height of aryballos on left 13 cm.

CHRISTIAN NUBIA
A.D. 550–1312

The Byzantine emperors, keen on acquiring allies in Nubia, sent missionaries to convert the local kings to Christianity, and by the late 6th century the kings of Nobatia in Lower Nubia, Makouria in Upper Nubia, and Alodia in Central Sudan had become Christian. Hundreds of churches and monasteries were built throughout the country, and their ruins still dot the Nile Valley. The **model of the Christian church at Adindan** (1150–1300) shows a typical structure. Such churches, and occasionally secular buildings, were decorated with colourful paintings depicting the Holy Family, saints, kings, and queens. Pottery, too, continued to be of high quality, and painted decoration featured such Christian motifs as crosses, doves, and fish.

Eye-paint (kohl) containers and applicators. Ivory, wood, and iron; from Gebel Adda (A.D. 200–550). Height of container on left 12 cm.

60

The Byzantine influence on Christian Nubia is apparent in the use of Greek in religious texts and on tomb stelae. Since the Nubian Church was headed by the patriarch of Alexandria, the use of Coptic, the language of Christian Egyptians, was also widespread. Following the example of the Meroites, however, the medieval Nubians invented their own writing system, by adapting Coptic characters to write the Nubian language. **Old Nubian texts,** both religious and secular, are found written on potsherds, vellum, and stone.

ISLAMIC NUBIA
A.D. 1312–1821

The Arab armies that conquered Egypt in the 7th century were stopped by the Nubians at the battle of Dongola in 652. The peace treaty signed between the kings of Nubia and the Moslem rulers of Egypt lasted for 600 years. Moslem merchants were allowed to trade in Nubia, and many of them apparently settled down in Nubian towns, given the evidence of the **Arabic tombstones** found at Gebel Adda. The Arab desert tribes also mingled with the Nubians. It was through this symbiotic coexistence and peaceful cultural contact that Nubians officially converted to Islam in the 14th century. The documents found at Gebel Adda and other sites suggest, however, that pockets of Christianity survived for at least another 150 years.

The earliest Islamic remains from Nubia date from the Christian period and presumably represent trade goods brought from Egypt and beyond. Beautiful **glazed pottery,** imported from Fatimid and Mameluke Egypt, is found at many Nubian sites.

The 1821 invasion of Nubia by the Turko-Egyptian army marks the division between the ancient and modern history of Nubia. The Islamic way of life continues to the present day.

MODERN NUBIA: CONTINUING TRADITIONS

The 20th century brought dramatic changes to the quiet life on the banks of the Nile. The total inundation of Lower Nubia, which resulted from the erection of the High Dam at Aswan, led to the resettlement of the population. Many of the ancient monuments were dismantled and relocated to new sites and museums. Nevertheless, large tracts of Nubia escaped destruction and many present-day Nubians continue their traditional way of life. It is still possible to find places where local artisans produce **leather goods, baskets, or musical instruments** similar to those made centuries ago.

Further Reading

Adams, William Y. *Nubia: Corridor to Africa*. 2nd ed. London: Allen Lane; Princeton: Princeton University Press, 1984.

Aldred, Cyril. *Egyptian Art in the Days of the Pharaohs, 3100–320 B.C.* New York: Oxford University Press, 1980.

——————. *The Egyptians*. London: Thames and Hudson, 1984.

Andrews, Carol. *Ancient Egyptian Jewellery*. London: British Museum Publications, 1980.

Baines, John, and Jaromír Málek. *Atlas of Ancient Egypt*. New York: Facts on File Publications, 1980.

Hobson, Christine. *The World of the Pharaohs*. New York: Thames and Hudson, 1987.

James, T. G. H. *An Introduction to Ancient Egypt*. London: British Museum Publications, 1979.

——————. *Pharaoh's People: Scenes from Life in Imperial Egypt*. London: The Bodley Head, 1984.

——————. *Ancient Egypt: The Land and Its Legacy*. Austin: University of Texas Press, 1988.

Kemp, Barry J. *Ancient Egypt: Anatomy of a Civilization*. London: Routledge, 1989.

el Mahdy, Christine. *Mummies, Myth, and Magic*. London: Thames and Hudson, 1989.

Säve-Söderbergh, Torgny. *Temples and Tombs of Ancient Nubia*. London: Thames and Hudson; Paris: UNESCO, 1987.

Taylor, John. *Egypt and Nubia*. London: British Museum Publications, 1991.